RED EYE FROG

A Practical Guide to Pet Ownership, Covering Habitat Setup, Nutrition, Health, Breeding and more..

Adams Jefferson

Table Of Contents

Introduction

1. Why Get a Pet Red Eye Frog?

For many reasons, getting a Red Eye Frog as a pet may be a fulfilling experience. First of all, they are an eye-catching addition to any house because to their remarkable look, which is distinguished by their vivid red eyes, brilliant green skin, and sometimes blue flanks or orange toes. In addition to their attractive appearance, Red Eye Frogs are renowned for their unusual habits, which provide life to their surroundings. These habits include exciting nighttime activities and unusual mating cries.

Second, Red Eye Frogs may be used as a teaching tool by adults and kids alike. In order to properly care for them, one must become knowledgeable about their nutrition, natural habitat, and the ecological function that they perform in the wild. This will help people appreciate biodiversity and the value of conservation. This may provide a better understanding of amphibians and the difficulties they encounter across the world.

Red Eye Frogs also provide an easy way to start a pastime for anyone who are interested in herpetology or the study of amphibians and reptiles.

As long as their unique food and environmental requirements are satisfied, they may be starters since their care requirements are simpler than those of other exotic pets. Taking care of them fosters accountability and may serve as a springboard for more advanced herpetological pursuits.

But it's crucial to remember that Red Eye Frogs need devotion, just like any other pet. To keep them healthy and happy, their habitat must replicate their natural surroundings, which involves keeping the right humidity and temperature levels and feeding them real insects. Red eye frogs may survive for many years with the right care, so prospective pet owners should be ready for the long-term commitment and everyday upkeep that comes with owning one.

2. Getting to Know Red-Eyed Frogs

The scientific name for red eye frogs is Agalychnis callidryas, and they are indigenous to the jungles of Central and South America. Their most distinguishing characteristic, their vivid red eyes, which are said to act as a protection mechanism against predators, is where their name originates. The frog wakes and opens its eyes when a predator gets close, maybe providing it an opportunity to flee by surprising the predator with its sudden bright eyes.

Since these frogs are nocturnal, nighttime is when they are most active. Their green backs serve as a disguise while they rest on the undersides of leaves throughout the day, only displaying their vivid colors when agitated. They eat mostly insects, including flies, moths, and crickets.

It is essential for anybody thinking about getting a Red Eye Frog as a pet to comprehend the species' natural habits and habitat requirements. They need a temperature range that is similar to their natural home in the tropical rainforest and a humid atmosphere. This usually entails putting up a terrarium with a heating arrangement to keep the temperature within an acceptable range and a misting system or frequent hand misting to maintain humidity.

Chapter One

Selecting a Red-Eyed Frog

1. Where Red Eye Frogs Can Be Found

When choosing a Red Eye Frog for a pet, there are a number of factors to take into account, with the main ones being the source's ethical and health standards. These are the main ways to locate a Red Eye Frog, along with some crucial factors to keep in mind for each.

Pet Stores: One easy place to locate Red Eye Frogs is a pet shop. On the other hand, frog health and circumstances might differ greatly across stores. Selecting a trustworthy retailer that upholds good standards of care for its animals is essential. Seek for establishments where the personnel is competent about caring for the animals, the enclosures are kept clean, and the animals seem lively and healthy.

Breeders: One of the greatest methods to locate a healthy Red Eye Frog is to buy straight from a breeder. Reputable breeders have a thorough understanding of the species and often provide comprehensive details on the frog's history of health issues, origins, and maintenance needs. They may also provide your pet with continuing assistance and guidance. Herpetological associations, amphibian enthusiast groups, and internet forums devoted to frog and reptile care are good places to start looking for breeders.

Expos and exhibits: Breeders and dealers congregate at reptile expos and exhibits to sell amphibians, reptiles, and associated goods. These gatherings provide a large variety of Red Eye Frogs as well as the chance to talk with the breeders personally about the upbringing and pedigree of their frogs. Additionally, they let you compare various frogs and settings side by side.

Rescue Centers: Another alternative is adoption via a rescue center or sanctuary. Red Eye Frogs who need new homes because their prior owners were unable to provide for them are sometimes taken care of by these facilities. Giving a frog a second shot at a happy life via adoption from a rescue facility may be satisfying. However, because of the frog's past circumstances, prospective owners should be ready to handle any health concerns or specific care needs.

internet Retailers: A large number of internet merchants focus on exotic animals, such as Red Eye Frogs. There are a lot of alternatives available when buying a frog online. But, it's crucial to do extensive research on the shop to make sure they use moral breeding and shipping practices. Examine evaluations and policies carefully about health warranties and live arrival assurances.

You should conduct extensive study before selecting a Red Eye Frog from any source. Recognize the unique requirements of Red Eye Frogs, set up the required environment ahead of time, and make sure you're prepared to devote yourself to their care. Inquiring about the frog's health, age, food, and past living circumstances may assist you in making an educated choice and locating a robust, healthy friend.

Choosing a Healthful Frog

A satisfying pet ownership experience begins with choosing a healthy Red Eye Frog. In addition to increasing the likelihood of flourishing in its new surroundings, a healthy frog lowers the possibility of spreading illnesses that might harm other pets or need expensive veterinarian care. These are some important clues to look for and questions to ask when choosing a Red Eye Frog so you can be sure the frog you bring home is healthy and active.

Examine Visually:

Eyes: A sound Red Eye Frog should have bright, clear eyes that are open all the way. Swollen, sunken, or cloudy eyes may be signs of underlying medical problems.

Skin: Search for moisturized, silky skin free of blemishes, extreme dryness, or discolouration. Unusual markings or abrasions may indicate inadequate hygiene or infection.

Activity Level: During their active phases, which are often at night, healthy frogs are normally aware and engaged. They should still move or blink in response to disruptions throughout the day.

Body Condition: The frog's body should be balanced, not too thin or swollen. An excessively bloated belly or visible ribs may be signs of health issues.

Behavior: Pay attention to the frog's actions. A frog in good health shouldn't show any indications of indifference or lethargic behavior. It ought to respond suitably to inputs.

Ask Questions:

Source: Find out the origin of the frog. Finding out whether it was captured in the wild or raised in captivity will help you prepare for any health concerns and difficulties adjusting.

Age: The frog's age might help you comprehend care requirements and behaviors unique to its life stage.

Diet: Discover the frog's recent feeding habits. Eating a proper, regular diet is essential to staying healthy.

Health History: Find out about any previous medical conditions or therapies the frog has had. This might include inquiries about injuries, diseases, or parasites.

Habitat: You may duplicate or enhance the frog's prior living circumstances in your own arrangement by being aware of them.

Environmental Concerns:

Quarantine: If you already have pets, think about how you'll quarantine the new frog to stop any possible infections from spreading.

Compatibility: To ensure that you offer an appropriate environment from the beginning, make sure you are informed of the frog's unique habitat demands, including temperature, humidity, and space.

Expert Health Exam: If at all feasible, have a veterinarian with a background in frogs do a prepurchase health examination. This may ease anxiety and reveal any problems that might not be apparent on a quick look.

Patience and careful consideration are necessary when choosing a healthy Red Eye Frog. The chances of a successful conclusion for you and your new pet are increased if you take the time to carefully examine the frog and ask the correct questions. Recall that the secret to a long and happy relationship with your Red Eye Frog is a good start.

Chapter Two

Establishing the Habitat

1. Requirements for Aquariums

An appropriate environment must be created for a Red Eye Frog to be healthy and happy. These frogs thrive best under conditions that are similar to the humidity, temperature, and vegetation of their native rainforest. Here's how to set up your Red Eye Frog in the right aquarium:

Depth and Room: A 10-gallon tank is the smallest size that is advised for a Red Eye Frog habitat that houses a single frog. Larger spaces, however, are usually preferable since they provide more room for enrichment and mobility. To avoid stress and overpopulation, if you want to maintain more than one frog, raise the tank capacity appropriately, adding 5–10 gallons each frog.

Substrate: The substrate, which is your aquarium's bottom layer, is essential for preserving humidity. Sphagnum moss, coconut fiber, or a combination of these plus soil are great options since they are safe for frogs and effectively retain moisture. Chips made of pine or cedar wood should be avoided since they may be poisonous to frogs.

Water Feature: Dechlorinated, pure water is necessary for Red Eye Frogs to survive. The frog may get water and a place to soak by adding a shallow water dish or making a little pond area in the aquarium. Since these frogs are not excellent swimmers, make sure the water is shallow enough to avoid drowning.

Humidity: Red Eye Frogs need high humidity levels, between 70 and 90 percent, to help them keep hydrated and replicate their native jungle habitat. For reliable humidity management, use a spray bottle to mist the cage once a day or use an automated misting system. You may keep an eye on the habitat's humidity levels with the use of a hygrometer.

Climatic: A Red Eye Frog's preferred habitat temperature ranges from 75–85°F (24–29°C) during the day, to 65–75°F (18–24°C) at night. Maintain these temperatures using an under-tank heater or a low-wattage heat lamp, and keep an eye on them with a thermometer placed within the tank. The tank should not be positioned in direct sunlight or next to windows as this might result in harmful temperature swings.

Illumination: Although they don't need specific UVB lighting, Red Eye Frogs benefit from having a natural light cycle that replicates day and night. To create 12 hours of light and 12 hours of darkness, use a low-intensity LED or fluorescent bulb. This may support their normal habits and assist control their circadian cycles.

Decorations and Plants: In addition to improving the habitat's look and humidity level, live plants provide your frog somewhere to hide and climb. Ferns, bromeliads, and pothos are examples of suitable plants. For added variety, use bark, smooth rocks, and driftwood into your landscaping. To avoid injuries, make sure all decorations are safe and devoid of sharp edges.

Maintenance and Cleaning: Frequent cleaning is necessary to stop the growth of dangerous fungus and germs. Spot-clean the habitat every day to get rid of trash and leftover food, and once a month, give it a more complete cleaning and switch out the substrate. Always rinse the cage well and use disinfectants appropriate for reptiles.

Your Red Eye Frog needs a suitable environment, so be sure to prepare ahead and pay close attention to the details. You may provide your amphibian pet with a pleasant and exciting environment that promotes their health and happiness by adhering to these aquarium criteria.

Humidity and Temperature

To replicate the natural rainforest home of your Red Eye Frog and to ensure its health and well-being, it is imperative that you keep its habitat at the proper temperature and humidity levels.

Temperature:

Range: During the day, a Red Eye Frog's environment should be between 75 and 85°F (24 and 29°C). To replicate the natural decrease in temperature they would encounter in the environment, it is helpful to slightly lower the temperature at night to 65–75°F (18–24°C). Their general health and metabolic activities are supported by this temperature range.

Control: To maintain these temperatures, use heating components such as low-wattage heat lamps, ceramic heat emitters, or under-tank heaters. To make sure there is a steady and suitable temperature gradient, place a thermometer at both the top and bottom of the tank.

Avoidance Measures: The tank should not be placed next to heaters, air conditioners, or windows since these external sources might cause abrupt temperature changes. To make sure the temperature stays within the intended range, check it often.

Humidity:

Levels: To simulate the wet atmosphere of a tropical rainforest, humidity levels should be kept between 70 and 90%. The frogs' skin health and level of hydration depend on this high humidity.

Maintenance: Install an automated misting system for more reliable humidity management, or use a spray bottle to mist the tank once a day. Another way to keep humidity levels in check in the habitat is to include a water element, such as a little pond or dish.

Monitoring: Check the humidity levels in the tank by inserting a hygrometer. To get a precise measurement of the total humidity in the tank, make sure it is positioned away from direct misting.

Greenery and Accents

By adding hiding places, climbing chances, and humidity control, real plants and ornaments to your

Red Eye Frog's environment not only improve its aesthetic appeal but also promote the frog's health and natural habits.

Flora:

Curation: Select non-toxic, humidity-loving plants that will flourish in the tank's environment. Bromeliads, orchids, ferns, and pothos are popular choices. In addition to creating a more realistic environment, these plants may aid in controlling the humidity in the tank.

Location: Plants should be arranged to provide depth and many hiding places for your frog in both the foreground and backdrop. To stop tall plants or branches from tipping over, make sure they are well secured.

Decorations:

Hiding Spots: Create climbing structures and hiding places using driftwood, smooth rocks, cork bark, and caverns. Red Eye Frogs value their capacity to conceal and withdraw as it helps them cope with stress.

Climbing Structures: Provide branches, vines, or bamboo poles for Red Eye Frogs to climb as they are arboreal. Exercise is also provided, and natural behavior is encouraged.

Security: To avoid unintentional harm, make sure all decorations are safely positioned and devoid of sharp edges. To prevent any openings or crevices where your frog may get trapped, take into account its size.

Extra Advice: Regularly check decorations and plants for wear or damage, and replace as needed. To avoid bringing pests or illnesses into the ecosystem, quarantine new plants or decorations before introducing them.

To provide more humidity and a natural floor covering that your frog will love for hiding and exploring, place a layer of leaf litter on top of the substrate.

You may create a cozy, engaging, and secure environment that closely resembles the Red Eye Frog's natural home, supporting their health and natural habits, by carefully controlling the temperature and humidity as well as choosing plants and decorations.

Chapter Three

Nutrition and Diet

1. What to Feed Your Red-Eyed Frog

Your Red Eye Frog's health and lifespan depend on feeding it a balanced diet and nutrients. Since these amphibians are insectivores, they mostly eat insects in the wild. To make sure they get all the nutrients they need in captivity, it's essential to replicate their natural diet as nearly as possible.

Food Types:

Primary Diet: Small to medium-sized insects like crickets, moths, flies, and mealworms should make up the majority of a Red Eye Frog's diet. Pet supply shops and internet vendors sell them. Feeding insects that are the right size for your frog is crucial; in general, the bug should not be bigger than the space between the frog's eyes.

Variety: Offer a range of insects to guarantee a well-rounded diet. You may avoid nutritional shortages and maintain your frog's interest in its meal by adding various kinds of insects.

Supplements: To make sure your frog gets all the nutrients it needs, particularly if your diet mostly consists of one kind of bug, dust the insects with a calcium supplement two to three times a week and a multivitamin supplement once a week. This is essential to avoid dietary deficit-related diseases such as metabolic bone disease.

Feeding Schedule:

Frequency: Juveniles should be fed daily because of their greater metabolic rate and growth requirements, however adults should normally be fed every other day.

Quantity: Your frog's age and size will determine how much food it needs. For an adult frog, giving it four to six appropriately sized insects every feeding session is an excellent place to start. Your frog should consume all food supplied within 15 minutes, so keep an eye on their hunger and make any necessary adjustments.

Timing: Red Eye Frogs are nocturnal, so feeding them in the evening is ideal when they're busiest. This may lead to more eager eating and is consistent with their normal hunting behavior.

Water: Always provide your frog access to a small dish of clean, dechlorinated water. Red Eye Frogs will often soak in the dish even if they may not drink from it directly, and the water helps keep the humidity in the environment stable. To keep the water clean and fresh, change it every day.

Feeding Tips:

Live Prey: Red Eye Frogs need to be fed live insects since they get their stimulation from moving prey.

Gut Loading: Feed your frog nourishing items to "gut load" them before introducing insects. Your frog will benefit from the enhanced nutritional content of the insects as a result of this treatment.

Observation: Make sure your frog is eating correctly and keep an eye on its health by often observing it during and after feeding. Appetite changes may be a precursor to health problems.

For your Red Eye Frog to be healthy, a proper food and nutrients are essential. Maintaining a regular feeding schedule and offering a diverse food along with essential vitamins can help you keep your pet frog healthy and happy.

Vitamins and Supplements

To replicate the variety of nutrients your Red Eye Frog would normally get from a broad range of food in the wild, you must add vitamins and minerals to their diet. It is difficult to duplicate this nutritional complexity in captivity without the need of supplements, even with a diversified diet. This is a comprehensive instruction explaining how to give your Red Eye Frog vitamins and nutrients.

Calcium:

Importance: Calcium is necessary for the health of amphibians' bones, muscles, and general metabolic functions. Metabolic bone disease is a dangerous disorder marked by weakening and abnormalities of the bones that may result from a deficit.

Supplementation: Before feeding the insects, sprinkle them with calcium supplements, which are often in the form of powder. For Red Eye Frogs, if your frog receives enough UVB sun, you should take a calcium supplement without vitamin D3, otherwise use one with vitamin D3. The frog can produce its own vitamin D3, which is required for the absorption of calcium, with the aid of UVB illumination. In the absence of UVB illumination, a calcium supplement containing vitamin D3 becomes necessary.

Frequency: To guarantee sufficient intake, dust prey with calcium two to three times each week.

Multivitamins:

Importance: A multivitamin supplement offers a variety of vitamins and minerals that support different body processes, such as digestion, reproduction, and immune system health. Vitamins A, B complex, C, D, and E are essential for amphibians.

Supplementation: Multivitamin supplements for frogs may be dust-applied to the insects in the same manner as calcium supplements. These supplements make sure your frog eats a healthy, balanced diet full of vital nutrients.

Recurrence: Apply a weekly multivitamin supplement to the prey. This frequency may change according on your frog's unique requirements and a veterinarian's recommendation.

Thoughts on Using Supplements:

1. Quality: Make sure the supplements you choose are safe and beneficial for your frog by selecting premium, reptile-specific brands.

2. Rotation: Follow the suggested timetable for switching between multivitamin and calcium supplements. To avoid the negative effects of both deficiencies and over-supplements, it's essential to strike the correct balance.

3. Gut Loading: Before giving the insects to your frog, gut load them for 24 to 48 hours to increase the efficiency of the supplements. Feeding the insects

nutrient-rich food allows them to transfer these nutrients to your frog, also known as gut loading.

4. meal Practices: To prevent waste and make sure the frog eats the powdered insects, apply supplements to a part of the insects at each meal. To promote consumption, you may also switch between feeding sessions with dusted and undusted insects.

5. Monitoring: Keep an eye out for indications that your frog is getting enough food by observing its behavior and general health. Frequent veterinarian examinations may assist in detecting any excesses or deficits in diet.

Chapter Four

Routine Upkeep and Care

1. Organizing the Habitat

For your Red Eye Frog to be healthy, it is imperative that you keep their environment clean. Maintaining a clean habitat lowers stress, prevents the growth of dangerous germs and fungus, and replicates the normal living circumstances of frogs. This is a comprehensive instruction on how to keep your Red Eye Frog's habitat clean and in good condition.

Daily Spot Cleaning:

What to Do: Take out any leftover food, waste, and excrement from the habitat every day. To make sure the water is always clean and fresh, check the water dish and replace the water every day.

Utilities to Apply: To remove waste, use a spoon or tiny net. In order to avoid cross-contamination, keep these instruments exclusive to the habitat.

Weekly Maintenance:

Substrate: Shake the substrate, depending on its kind, to get rid of any waste that is visible and to stop mold from growing. It's possible that certain substrates need replacement more often than others.

Water Features: To stop the spread of germs and algae, clean and replace the water in your habitat once a week if it has a small pond or waterfall.

Decorations and Plants: Take down any decorations and plants, and look for any indications of pollution or rotting. Before returning them to their environment, give them any essential cleanings.

Monthly Deep Cleaning:

Complete Habitat Cleaning: Clean the whole habitat thoroughly once a month. In order to do this, the frog must be taken to a secure, temporary cage, and the environment must then be thoroughly cleaned.

Disinfection: Clean the tank, decorations, and other non-living components using a disinfectant suitable for reptiles. Make sure you completely rinse everything with water to get rid of any remaining cleaning chemical residue.

Substrate Replacement: To guarantee a clean foundation for the habitat, replace the substrate completely. To limit the development of waste and germs, a full replacement is required, even with frequent stirring and spot cleaning of the substrate.

Equipment Check: Examine and clean any habitat-related equipment, including lighting, humidifiers, and heaters. Make sure they are operating securely and properly.

Overall Advice:

Health: To stop the transmission of germs and parasites, always wash your hands before and after touching your frog or cleaning the habitat.

Temporary Housing: Make sure your frog has a safe and secure temporary home while the cleaning is being done. It should have enough ventilation, the right temperature and humidity, and, if necessary, lengthier cleaning sessions.

Habitat Drying: After cleaning and before reinstating your frog, let the habitat air dry fully. This reduces the possibility of skin or respiratory disorders.

Observation: Watch your frog's behavior to make sure it adapts to the changes well after cleaning and reorganizing the environment. By creating hiding spots and reducing disturbances, you may speed up the frogs' acclimation process, since some may get anxious following habitat disturbances.

The secret to avoiding illness and providing your Red Eye Frog with a healthy, engaging environment is routinely and thoroughly cleaning its habitat. Your frog may have a long and healthy life if you follow a regular cleaning routine and use safe, suitable cleaning techniques.

Tracking Well-Being

It's essential to monitor your Red Eye Frog's health closely in order to identify and address any possible problems early on. Frequent observation enables you to see indicators of disease, suffering, or environmental issues in the frog's habitat that might be detrimental to its health. Here's how to keep an accurate tab on your Red Eye Frog's health:

Outward Appearance :

Skin: Examine skin for lesions, discolorations, and unusual shedding. A healthy frog should have moist, smooth skin that shows no symptoms of illness or discomfort.

Eyes: The eyes need to be bright, open, and clear. Swelling, cloudiness, or persistent closure may be signs of illness.

Physical State: Seek indications of a healthy weight—one that is neither too lean nor bloated. If a frog has an enlarged belly or seems malnourished, it can be ill.

Activity Level: Red eye frogs in good health are usually active at night. Even if they are not moving much throughout the day, they should react to disruptions.

Behavioral Signals:

Eating: Take note of any variations in hunger. An abrupt loss of appetite may indicate a medical condition or stress.

Movement: Pay attention to how the frog moves. Lethargy, trouble leaping, or an odd stride may be signs of health issues.

Breathing: Keep an eye out for any indications of difficult breathing or frequent mouth opening, since these might point to respiratory problems.

Environmental Checks:

Humidity and Temperature: Make sure that the habitat's humidity and temperature are within the range that Red Eye Frogs like. Deviations might cause stress and other health issues for your frog.

Cleanliness: Make sure the frog's environment is clear of mildew, fungus, and excessive trash, since these might host infections that could be detrimental to it.

Daily Routine Health Assessments: Regular Observations: Integrate health examinations into your everyday schedule. Knowing your frog's typical look and activity can help you recognize abnormalities more easily.

Veterinarian Visits: Make an appointment for routine examinations with a veterinarian who specializes in the care of frogs. They can address any worries you may have and provide expert health examinations.

New Items Under Quarantine: To stop the transmission of illness, you should always quarantine new frogs or other animals before bringing them into the environment of your current pet.

When to Seek Veterinary Care: See a veterinarian as soon as possible if you see any of the above-mentioned symptoms of disease or distress. For many amphibian health conditions to be effectively treated, early intervention is essential.

Proactive Steps: Nutrition and Supplements: Make sure your frog eats a well-balanced diet and supplements that include the vitamins and minerals it needs to maintain good health.

Reduction of Stress: Reduce stress by giving your frog a good home, treating it gently (if at all), and keeping the surroundings steady.

It takes regular observation and proactive care to keep an eye on your Red Eye Frog's health. You may contribute to ensuring your pet lives a long, healthy life by being watchful and acting swiftly in the event of any health difficulties.

Chapter Five

Managing and Communicating

1. How to Treat Your Frog Properly

Like any other amphibian, a red eye frog should be handled carefully and with consideration for its welfare. Because of their highly absorbable skin, which is porous, amphibians may be especially sensitive to stress, injury, and exposure to toxins from human skin. Here's how to care for your Red Eye Frog safely:

Reduce Handling: First and foremost, it's critical to understand that the majority of frogs, particularly Red Eye Frogs, dislike being touched. Handling often might lead to stress and health problems. Only handle your frog when absolutely required, as during veterinarian appointments or habitat maintenance.

Wash Your Hands: Thoroughly wash your hands with water and a light soap before touching your frog. Rinse carefully to get rid of any soap residue. To get rid of any oils, salts, or possibly dangerous materials from your skin, this step is essential. As an alternative, think about putting on disposable gloves that have been moistened to provide a barrier between your skin and the frog. Make sure there are no lubricants or powders on the gloves.

Establish a Moist Environment: Gently pick up the frog by wetting your hands with dechlorinated water. The wetness imitates the frog's natural, humid habitat while also protecting its skin.

Careful Handling: Use a light, delicate touch to pick up your frog. Raise the frog up from underneath and let it settle into the palm of your hand. Gently press it there with your fingers. Refrain from holding or squeezing excessively firmly since this may result in harm or discomfort.

When handling, keep the frog near a soft surface in case it tries to leap away. This might be placed within the cage itself to reduce the chance of damage from a fall, or it could be placed over a table or bed.

Limit Exposure Time: To reduce stress, handle sessions briefly. It should just take a few minutes to complete the essential activities.

After Handling: To get rid of any germs or materials the frog could have left on your skin, wash your hands once more after handling.

Inform Others: Should friends or relatives show an interest in cuddling your frog, inform them of the need for minimum, delicate handling and watch over any interactions to guarantee the frog's security.

Watch Your Frog : After handling, keep an eye out for any indications of stress or pain on your frog. A change in color, a decrease in activity, or an appetite loss are other symptoms. If you see any worrisome signs, minimize handling even further and seek veterinary advice if required.

It's important to strike a balance between the frog's health and stress levels and the need for contact while caring for your Red Eye Frog. You may make sure that any essential handling is done with the least amount of danger to your pet amphibian by according to these rules.

Comprehending the Behavior of Your Frog

It's crucial to comprehend your Red Eye Frog's natural habits and what they could mean about its habitat, health, and emotions in order to protect its wellbeing and provide it the finest care possible. Here's a thorough analysis of typical Red Eye Frog actions along with interpretations:

Activities at Night: Red Eye Since frogs are typically nocturnal, nighttime is when they are most active. They prefer to hide behind leaves or in other protected areas of their environment during the day, when they are most active. If your frog is active during the day, it might indicate a stress-related condition or a problem with the lighting or other aspects of the environment.

Vocalizations: Males often emit vocalizations, particularly at night. These sounds may be a component of their territorial or mating call. If your frog makes these noises, it usually indicates that it is comfortable where it is. On the other hand, if the habitat is not properly set up or if there are too many frogs in a confined area, excessive vocalization may also be a sign of stress.

Closing: Red Eye Frogs often look for hiding spots where they may feel comfortable and protected. Enough hiding places in their ecosystem are essential to their survival. Constant concealment might also be a sign of stress or discomfort in their surroundings, perhaps brought on by unfavorable lighting, temperature, or predator presence.

Ascents and Descents: Red Eye Frogs are arboreal animals that love to climb. You may find them on the edges of their cage or on the plants and branches that are part of their natural environment. Jumping is another instinctive activity. Frequent, hysterical leaping against the enclosure walls, however, might be a sign of stress or an effort to flee inappropriate surroundings.

Dining Routines: An insatiable hunger is a sign of a healthy Red Eye Frog. Refusal to eat may indicate medical conditions, stress, or problems with the recommended diet. It's critical to keep an eye on their eating patterns and make sure they're getting a balanced diet that meets their nutritional requirements.

Shedding Skin: As a normal part of their growing process, frogs regularly lose their skin. It's possible that you've seen your frog consume its lost skin, which is natural and aids in their nutritional recovery. Incomplete or difficult sheds may be a sign of health problems or unfavorable habitat circumstances.

hue Changes: Stress levels, humidity, temperature, and general health may all affect a red eye frog's hue. Although little fluctuations in hue are natural, large or abrupt shifts might be an indication of disease, stress, or problems with the temperature.

Dampling: It's normal to see your frog submerged in its water dish, especially in the days leading up to shedding or during very dry spells. It facilitates the shedding process and keeps them moisturized. Make sure there are no hazards for drowning, such as dirty, shallow water.

Creating a caring environment that satisfies your Red Eye Frog's demands requires that you comprehend and understand its behavior. Your frog may have a happy and healthy life if you watch out for these habits and react properly to any symptoms of suffering or disease. If you see any alarming

changes in behavior or health, always seek the
advice of a veterinarian skilled in amphibian care.

Chapter Six

Well-being and Health

1. Common Medical Conditions

Like any other pet, red eye frogs might have specific health problems. By being aware of the telltale signs and symptoms of these typical issues, you might possibly save your frog's life by seeking prompt medical treatment. Here's a thorough look at some of the most typical health problems Red Eye Frogs encounter:

Infections by Bacteria and Fungi: Symptoms: Skin redness, swelling, lesions, or discoloration; fatigue; appetite loss.

Causes: The frog's immune system may be strained by low or high temperatures, poor water quality, and poor cleanliness, which increases the frog's susceptibility to diseases.

Prevention/Medication: Ensure that the environment is kept tidy and well-conditioned. See a veterinarian for a diagnosis and treatment plan that may include antifungal or antibiotic drugs.

Metabolic Bone Disease (MBD): Symptoms: Weakness, sluggishness, spinal or limb abnormalities, trouble moving.

Causes: Inadequate calcium-to-phosphorus ratio in the diet, vitamin D3 inadequacy, or calcium deficiency.

Prevention/Medication: Make sure your food is well-balanced and that calcium and vitamin D3 are included. Frogs may also naturally produce vitamin D3 with the aid of UVB lighting. A veterinarian may provide treatment alternatives, including as

food modifications and supplements, if MBD is
detected.

Parasitic Infections:

Symptoms: bloating, tiredness, abnormal feces,
weight loss despite regular eating.

Causes: Inadequate hygiene or tainted food might
introduce parasites.

Prevention/Treatment: Many parasite illnesses may
be avoided with good hygiene and routine habitat
cleaning. Depending on the kind of illness, a
veterinarian may diagnose and provide antiparasitic
medications.

Obesity: Symptoms: Increased body weight, trouble
moving about.

Causes: Overfeeding, particularly when it involves
high-fat meals, or a diet deficient in diversity.

Prevention/Medication: Keep an eye on food
consumption, make sure the diet is balanced, and

create an environment that promotes exercise and natural motions.

Infections of the Respiratory System: Significance: Difficulty breathing, fatigue, mucous in the mouth or nose.

Causes: Respiratory problems might arise as a result of inadequate ventilation, low temperatures, or excessive humidity.

Prevention/Treatment: Make sure enough ventilation is in place, and maintain the proper humidity and temperature levels. Antibiotics may be prescribed by a veterinarian to treat respiratory infections caused by bacteria.

Problems with Shedding Skin:
Symptoms: Partially shed skin that adheres to the body.

Causes: Dietary deficits or low humidity.

Prevention/Treatment: Make sure the environment has the right amount of humidity. Adding necessary vitamins and minerals to the diet might also be beneficial. If there is just partial skin shedding, speak with a veterinarian about the safe removal of the remaining skin.

Chemical Toxicity:

Symptoms: Quick onset of unconsciousness, seizures, or fatality.

Reasons: chemical exposure via cleaning products, tainted water, or hand residue handling.

Prevention/Medication: When cleaning the habitat, use only materials that are suitable for frogs and make sure to rinse everything well. For the habitat, use dechlorinated water, and wet your hands before handling. If poisoning is thought to be present, get veterinary help right away.

You may maintain your Red Eye Frog's health by identifying the early warning symptoms of these conditions, learning about their causes, and taking preventative measures. A healthy diet, frequent health examinations, and keeping a tidy and suitable atmosphere are essential. Before beginning any therapy, always seek the advice of a veterinarian with expertise in caring for amphibians if you have any health concerns.

Health Promotion

Your Red Eye Frog's long-term health and wellbeing depend on receiving preventative treatment. You may reduce your pet's risk of disease and provide a healthy environment for them by being proactive in preventing illness. The following are thorough methods for providing quality preventive care:

Correct Habitat Configuration and Upkeep:
Humidity and Temperature: Sustain the proper humidity levels (70-90%) and temperature ranges (75-85°F during the day, slightly lower at night) for Red Eye Frogs. Utilize a thermometer and hygrometer to routinely check these parameters.
Cleanliness: Keep the habitat clean on a regular basis by changing the substrate and doing weekly thorough cleanings in addition to daily spot checks for trash and uneaten food, as well as weekly inspections of the water features. This inhibits the development of bacteria and fungi.
Ventilation: Make sure there is enough ventilation in the habitat to stop the growth of dangerous infections.

Well-Balanced Nutrition and Supplementation:
Diet: Provide a variety of insects of the right size to satisfy dietary requirements and avoid obesity. Don't overindulge in food.

Supplements: To avoid metabolic bone disease and other nutritional deficiencies, sprinkle meals with calcium and vitamin supplements on a regular basis. If you don't have UVB illumination in your setup, use calcium and vitamin D3.

Gut Loading: To increase the nutritional value of the insects, feed them a healthy meal for 24 to 48 hours prior to giving them to your frog.

UVB Lighting: UVB lighting may help with vitamin D3 production, which is important for calcium absorption, if your setup permits it. To avoid stressing the frog, make sure the lighting isn't too harsh and that it may hide in regions with shade.

Quarantine additional Additions: To stop the transmission of parasites or illnesses, quarantine any additional frogs or live food sources for a minimum of 30 days before adding them to your current setup.

Regular Health Monitoring:

Visual Checks: Keep an eye out for any changes in behavior, appetite, skin condition, or activity level that might indicate an illness, injury, or suffering in your frog.

Veterinary Care: Make an appointment for regular check-ups and develop a connection with a veterinarian who specializes in amphibian care. They can address any problems before they become worse and provide insightful guidance on food, hygiene, and environmental management.

Minimize Handling: Minimize handling to relax tension and lower the chance of being hurt or spreading illness. Before touching your frog or cleaning the environment, always wash your hands.

Stress Reduction: Reduce stress, which may impair immunity, by creating a calm atmosphere and plenty of hiding places. Steer clear of possible stressors including unexpected movements and loud sounds.

Water Quality: Use filtered or dechlorinated water for the water features and habitat. Amphibians may be harmed by pollutants like chlorine and other substances often present in tap water.

Education and Awareness : Remain aware of the requirements for Red Eye Frog care, and take the initiative to find out information from reliable sources such as care manuals, forums for amphibian lovers, and experts in amphibian care.

You can provide your Red Eye Frog a secure and healthy habitat, lower their risk of health problems, and ensure they live long, happy lives by putting these preventive care tips into practice.

Chapter Seven

Breeding Frogs with Red Eyes

1. The Method of Breeding

It may be a satisfying experience to breed Red Eye Frogs (Agalychnis callidryas) in captivity, but it does involve careful preparation, the right habitat, and knowledge of their breeding habits. The Red Eye Frog breeding procedure is explained in full below:

Readiness for Mating:
Sexual Development: Make sure your frogs are ready for reproduction before trying to mate them. Red Eye Frogs usually need 1-2 years to attain sexual maturity.

Healthy Pair: Choose two fit people to breed. They should have received the best care possible and show no symptoms of illness or stress.

Conditioning: Give the frogs high-quality, nutrient-rich food before mating. By doing this, you can make sure they're in optimal health for mating and producing eggs.

Creating a Suitable Environment: Enclosure Setup: Construct a rain chamber or make modifications to the current enclosure to replicate the circumstances of the rainy season, which incite Red Eye Frogs to reproduce. Increasing humidity and changing the illumination to simulate longer days may be two ways to do this.

Temperature: Keep the temperature at the Red Eye Frog's preferred range; at night, keep it a little lower to replicate the environment.

Featured Water: Add a pool or small section of water to the enclosure so that eggs may be laid there. Both pure and dechlorinated water are required.

Hiding Spots and Vegetation: To provide the frogs a safe and pleasant habitat, add plenty of plants, both genuine and fake.

Starting the Breeding Process:

Simulating Rainy Season: Mist the enclosure more regularly by hand or with a misting device to replicate the rainy season and promote breeding behavior.

Increased Feeding: Give the frogs more food to make sure they have enough energy for mating.

Observation: Keep an eye out for signs of romance. The frogs may be more active and communicate with one another, and males may call to entice females.

Egg Laying and Fertilization:

Egg Laying: Depending on the configuration, the female will lay eggs directly in the water or on the underside of leaves. As the eggs are deposited, the male externally fertilizes them.

Egg Care: To keep the eggs from drying out, make sure they are kept in a humid atmosphere. If placed on leaves, you may need to lightly spray.

Tadpole Care:

Hatching: Depending on temperature and circumstances, eggs will hatch into tadpoles in a period of one to ten days.

Feeding Tadpoles: Commercial tadpole food, boiled vegetables (like lettuce), or algae may be given to tadpoles as food. Maintain the purity and oxygenation of the water.

Development: Track the tadpoles' growth and the start of their transition into froglets. The tadpoles will progressively grow legs and absorb their tails throughout this process, which may take many months.

Bringing Up Froglets:

Transition: Tadpoles must have access to land regions in their aquatic habitat as they change into froglets.

Tadpole Care: Froglets may initially continue to eat tadpole food, but as they become bigger, they will progressively switch to a diet of tiny insects.

Red eye frog breeding need for perseverance and meticulous attention to detail. Throughout the process, it's critical to keep an eye on the frogs' and their young's growth and health, adjusting their care as necessary. Raising Red Eye Frogs successfully may help with knowledge and conservation of this species while providing insightful information about their amazing life cycle.

Preserving Tadpoles

Raising healthy Red Eye Frogs requires completing the important task of tadpole care. To guarantee the tadpoles grow into froglets in the correct manner, there are certain nutritional, environmental, and health issues throughout this phase. This is a thorough tutorial on tadpole maintenance:

Habitat Setup:
Tank Conditions: Provide the tadpoles with an appropriate aquatic habitat. A small group of tadpoles can fit in a 10-gallon tank, but bigger groups will need a larger area. Prior to adding the tadpoles, make sure the tank is clean.
Water Quality: Fill the tank with aged or dechlorinated tap water. Tadpoles of Red Eye Frogs prefer a temperature range of 72–78°F (22–25°C). If required, use a water heater, and have an aquarium

thermometer handy to keep an eye on the temperature.

Filtration: To maintain clean water without producing powerful currents that can stress tadpoles, use a light filtration system. For this, sponge filters are perfect.

Aeration: Use an air stone or a mild filter output to make sure the water is adequately oxygenated. For a healthy growth, tadpoles need water with enough oxygen content.

Nutrition and Feeding:

Timetable for Feeding: Small portions of food should be given to tadpoles two to three times a day; avoid overfeeding as this might contaminate the water. After a few hours, remove any uneaten food to preserve the water's purity.

Diet: The main foods for tadpoles are algae and plant material. Serve them commercial tadpole food, boiled and chopped leafy greens (lettuce or spinach), or algal wafers. Add little bits of meals strong in protein, such as cooked egg yolk or premium fish flakes, as they mature and begin to sprout legs.

Water Maintenance:

Partial Water Changes: To preserve water quality, do weekly partial water changes, changing around 20–25% of the tank water. To prevent stunning the tadpoles, take care to adjust the pH and temperature of the new water to the surrounding circumstances. Cleaning: During water changes, use a siphon to remove waste and uneaten food from the bottom of the tank. Keep any chemicals and soaps out of the tadpole tank and its surroundings.

Development Monitoring:

Size and Modifications: Track the tadpoles' growth, noticing the emergence of legs and the gradual thinning of the tail. Depending on the species and environment, the change from tadpole to froglet might take from weeks to months.

Adjustments to Habitat: Add tiny, flat pebbles or a ramp to provide the tadpoles easy access to places where they may rest out of the water when they start to grow legs and spend more time at the surface.

Health Considerations:

Observation: Keep an eye out for any symptoms of disease or discomfort, such as lethargy, lack of appetite, or strange swimming patterns, by regularly checking the tadpoles.

Clean Environment: Reducing bacterial and fungal infections, which are frequent problems that might harm tadpoles, requires regular tank cleaning.

Transition to Froglets: Diet Transition: Tadpoles must switch to a diet of tiny insects, including flightless fruit flies or pinhead crickets, in order to mirror their carnivorous adult diet.

Terrestrial Areas: Since the froglets will need to breathe air, make sure the tank contains places where they may completely depart the water.

Tadpoles need careful consideration of their surroundings, food, and overall health while receiving care. You may effectively raise tadpoles into healthy adult frogs by giving them a clean, stable home, giving them the right diet, and keeping an eye on their growth. This worthwhile procedure provides a rare chance to see the amazing Red Eye Frog life cycle.

Chapter Eight

Troubleshooting Typical Problems

Like any pet, Red Eye Frog ownership might provide some difficulties. Maintaining the health and happiness of your frog depends on your ability to recognize and resolve frequent problems. Here are thorough explanations and fixes for some of the most typical issues that Red Eye Frog owners go across.

1. Frog Not Eating:

Potential Causes: Stress, sickness, unsuitable meal size, or incorrect tank conditions (temperature, humidity).

Remedies: Check and set the habitat's humidity and temperature to the appropriate values. Offer a range of meal portions that are suitable in size. See a veterinarian if the frog continues to avoid food since this might indicate a medical condition.

2. Skin Issues (Infections, Shedding Problems): Potential Causes: Inappropriate humidity or low water quality might result in bacterial or fungal infections. Low humidity might lead to incomplete shedding.
Remedies: Maintain a cleaner environment and replace the water often. Mist more often to regulate humidity. To get the right care for chronic skin conditions or suspected infections, see a veterinarian.

3. Constantly Hiding, Reduced Activity—Signs of Stress: Potential Causes: Insufficient hiding places, excessive handling, combative tankmates, or inappropriate tank conditions.

Remedies: Minimize handling and make sure there are plenty of plants and hiding places in the tank. Check compatibility between tank mates. As necessary, check and modify the humidity and temperature settings.

4. Atypical Conduct (Heavy Leaping, Screaming): Possible Origins: Stress, an effort to get out of bad circumstances, or, in the case of vocalizing, an instinctive breeding action.
Remedies: Make sure the tank has the right temperatures, enough room, and is secure and maintained. Particularly in men, excessive vocalization without other indications of stress may be considered typical behavior.

5. Problems with Water Quality: Possible Causes: Inadequate filtration, overfeeding, and irregular water changes.

Remedies: To stop decay and degradation of the water quality, do routine water changes, make sure the filtering system is sufficient for the tank size, and remove any uneaten food right away.

6. Disease of the Metabolic Bone:
Potential Causes: inadequate UVB illumination, a diet deficient in calcium and vitamin D3.
Remedies: Add calcium and vitamin D3 to the diet. If UVB illumination isn't already being used, think about supplying it. You should also speak with a veterinarian about treatment options and dietary changes.

7. Respiratory Infections: Potential Causes: High humidity, extreme cold, or inadequate ventilation. Remedies: Make sure there is enough ventilation and that the habitat's temperature and humidity are adjusted to the proper levels. In the event that a

bacterial infection is identified, a veterinarian may prescribe antibiotics.

Overall Troubleshooting Advice: Daily Observation: Pay careful attention to your frog's actions, hunger, and physical attributes. Effective therapy depends on early problem discovery.

Veterinary treatment: Form a rapport with a vet who specializes in the treatment of frogs. They may provide priceless guidance and therapeutic alternatives.

Become Informed: Keep up your education on Red Eye Frog maintenance to make sure you're giving them the greatest habitat possible.

You can keep your Red Eye Frog happy and healthy by being aware of these typical problems and learning how to solve them. To prevent more stress, always make adjustments gradually and keep an eye on how they are affecting your frog.